BY
Elfreda Powell

PARRAGON

This edition first published by
Parragon Book Service Ltd in 1996

Parragon Book Service Ltd
Unit 13–17 Avonbridge Trading Estate
Atlantic Road, Avonmouth
Bristol BS11 9QD

Produced by Magpie Books,
an imprint of Robinson Publishing

ISBN 0 75251 792 9

A copy of the British Library Cataloguing in Publication
Data is available from the British Library.

Typeset by Whitelaw & Palmer Ltd, Glasgow

'The fathomless deep. Huge emotions right under the surface,' is how Meryl Streep describes his eyes. Dark, enigmatic and brooding, Robert De Niro is one of America's finest contemporary actors and has been compared to both Marlon Brando and Alec Guinness. He chooses his role with care: his characters come from the flipside of the American Dream, from the urban underworld, the garishly lit streets, the boxing ring, the casino, the heist; they are people who live on the edge, in a world of violence.

He is a perfectionist, he becomes his role with total commitment, then stands back slightly, relaxes, so that after his performance we emerge from the cinema thinking and seeing the way *his* characters think and see.

On the subject of his private life, he is reserved. Newsweek magazine called him 'a black hole'. His evasive, inarticulate interviews give almost nothing away. His girl-friends are kept secret; his family life is his personal affair; his circle of friends is small. He does not want to be recognised in the street.

Director Brian De Palma calls him 'a chameleon', for his ability to change totally with every role, donning that persona, *becoming* that person, so much so that we might be

forgiven for asking: Where is the real De
Niro? Who is he escaping from?

# A LONELY CHILDHOOD

Robert De Niro grew up in New York's Greenwich Village. His father, who had the same name, was an idealist, a painter of such high standards that before he would sell a painting, he had to think that the buyer was worthy of buying it. As a consequence, much of his life was spent on the breadline. He was born in Syracuse, New York, of an Italian father and Irish mother, and studied painting at classes run by Hans Hofmann – an Abstract Expressionist painter who had fled Nazi

4

Germany and become the central figure in the contemporary art movement in the east of the United States.

It was at Hans Hofmann's classes that Robert De Niro Sr met his future wife, a girl from Oregon called Virginia Admiral. She was equally talented as a painter. They fell in love, married, and went to live in Greenwich Village, at that time a lively centre of bohemian life.

Their only child, Robert, was born on 17 August 1943. By all accounts they were a happy, but rather intense couple, who joined in the life around them: Greenwich Village was full of struggling artists like themselves, would-be writers and musicians, actors and intellectuals, and of course the usual number of fakes. They were to meet their nemesis in one of the latter – a quack psychoanalyst, who persuaded them, as he had persuaded a number of other couples, that they were not really happy together and should split up. So when Robert De Niro was only two years old, his parents went their separate ways.

His father continued to live from hand to mouth, struggling to make his way as an artist, moving from one dank loft to another; his mother, however, could no longer afford such an idealised way of life – she had to earn some money. She started her own small business, doing secretarial work and proof-reading. Robert's parents' separation was not rancorous, and they continued to be on reasonable terms, although they divorced when Robert was only four in 1948.

With his mother preoccupied with her work,

and as an only child, Robert, or Bobby as he is
generally known, was a solitary child, very
reliant on his own resources. He enjoyed
reading, and also looked forward to the time
he spent with his father, which, by all
accounts, included visits to cinemas. His father
had a volatile personality, and the high standards he demanded of himself were also
extended to those around him. De Niro's own
perfectionism as an actor undoubtedly had its
roots in his relationship with his father. When
Bobby was eight, his father disappeared completely from his life for four years – he decided
to try to make his living as an artist in post-war
France, but had no more success there.

Bobby attended the local school in Greenwich
Village. He was reputedly very shy and intro-
verted, and fared only moderately well in class.
He played truant but didn't join any street

gangs and certainly wasn't tough – he preferred reading a book. However, he was persuaded to take part in the school play, leading to his first public appearance as an actor – as the Cowardly Lion in *The Wizard of Oz*. Putting on a disguise is a way for a shy child to gain courage, and it was obviously something he enjoyed.

One of Virginia De Niro's clients ran a famous drama school. This was the Dramatic Workshop directed by Erwin and Marie Ley Piscator. Many celebrated actors had passed through its doors including Marlon Brando in the early 1940s, who, in the 1950s, was mesmerising theatre and cinema audiences with his performances. At the age of ten, Bobby enrolled in their speech and drama classes.

By the time he was thirteen, his mother could

afford to send him to a private school, but he still didn't shine academically and left at sixteen. Already, he seemed to know exactly what he wanted to do – he wanted to act in films. He had been inspired, it would seem, not so much by actors of the moment such as Brando, Montgomery Clift and James Dean, but by the films *Can-Can*, *The Thing* and *Invasion of the Body Snatchers*. He joined the Stella Adler Conservatory of Acting to further his dream and studied there for three years.

Stella Adler had formerly worked at Piscator's school and was a great teacher. Brando acknowledges her as the most formative influence in his life. She had studied under Stanislavsky at the Moscow Arts Theatre, and had brought back his technique of Method acting to the States. Brando had been the first to bring Method acting successfully to the screen in

*The Men* and *A Streetcar Named Desire,* and all young aspiring actors were now copying his technique.

Adler taught actors to study outward clues to the character they were playing, as well as to replicate the character's emotions by looking inwards and finding parallel emotions or situations in their past that could provoke similar reactions. She taught restrained vocal expression, advocating understatement – a subtlety in technique much suited to the screen and one that would revolutionise film-making, in particular bringing greater sensitivity and power to the close-up.

There was a rivalry between Adler and a fellow teacher of the Method – Lee Strasberg – who had established himself at the Actors Studio, where De Niro next attended workshop sessions, but never enrolled as a student. Strasberg laid even more emphasis on using past feelings and past experiences to conjure up the emotions of a character, and De Niro was able to plunder his painful past to good effect. Strasberg immediately recognised his talent and encouraged it, although it would be many years before De Niro achieved public recognition.

# WAITING IN THE WINGS

De Niro continued living in the Greenwich Village area, although it had lost its former bohemian glamour. His father had returned to France, but was found to be living at starvation level, so Bobby set off for Paris to bring him home. He says little about this episode except that it was 'a nightmare'. His mother, on the other hand, had taken up painting again and was now having some success. The Museum of Modern Art in New York would eventually buy one of her paintings – no small achievement.

It was in the early 1960s that Bobby managed to get his first film audition with Brian de Palma, for *The Wedding Party*, although it would not be the break he was hoping for. De Palma found him intensely shy, but offered him a small part, which De Niro gladly accepted, thinking that the salary was $50 a week, and not, as it turned out, a flat fee of $50 for several weeks' filming. Worse still, the film would not be released for another six years, when it promptly sank without trace.

De Niro didn't make another film for some years, and in the meantime, worked hard at perfecting his craft. A girlfriend, Sally Kirkland, said that he had created a portfolio of 25 very different characters, whose inspiration had come from novels he'd read. And he took part in any small theatre production that he could find: from Chekhov and Eugene O'Neill to a German Expressionist play. One of his more fascinating theatre appearances was in *Glory, Glamour and Gold*, a production well off-Broadway featuring Candy Darling, a transvestite friend of the Pop artist, Andy Warhol. While Candy did Marilyn Monroe impersonations, De Niro partnered him/her in no less than five different roles.

After this, De Niro took another trip to Europe – this time hitch-hiking in search of his Irish and Italian roots. He managed to track down the Italian side of his family in the hill town of Campobasso, some fifty miles from Naples.

When he returned to New York, he made his second appearance on film – in a walk-on part in Marcel Carné's *Trois Chambres à Manhattan*, and not long after that was invited by Brian De Palma to take part in two further unmemorable counter-culture films: *Greetings* and its sequel, *Hi, Mom!*. Both had plenty of sex and violence. In the first he played someone pretending to be a right-wing militant to avoid being called-up for Vietnam (the war was by then in its third year). He changed his physical appearance so successfully that De Palma failed to recognise him. In *Hi, Mom!*, he became a voyeur.

Although De Niro was still reserved and self-effacing, once he had immersed himself in his role, he was transformed. He saw life entirely through the eyes of his character. It was as though acting gave him permission to do things he would never dare do himself. And De Palma encouraged him to improvise.

Sally Kirkland introduced him to Shelley Winters, by then a well-established star who had made some 50 films. She recognised his 'sexual lightning' on stage, and took him under her wing, becoming his 'Jewish Mama', and a true, lifelong friend. She obtained a part for him in a satirical play, as a bisexual Method actor who is also a karate expert. De Niro had karate training for three weeks, and by the time the play was staged, could chop a piece of wood in two with his bare hand. Although the play was a flop, De Niro was noticed.

Several more 'dogs' followed – *Sam's Song*, *Jennifer on My Mind* and *Born to Win* (the latter two films about drugs – by then a hackneyed theme), and *The Gang that Couldn't Shoot Straight*, in which he played what was for him a seminal role – as an Italian gangster. He was scrupulous about his research and set off to

Mother and sons, *Bloody Mama*

Calabria in the south of Italy with a tape-recorder to get his accent absolutely right. Although the film was slated, De Niro's performance was picked out for special mention.

It was 1969 before De Niro first appeared in a commercial film – *Bloody Mama* – albeit a B-movie with a poor script. Its director-producer, Roger Corman, liked mixing unknown talent with better known actors, and Shelley Winters, playing Ma Baker, matriarch of a 1930's family of thugs, had helped him to get a role as one of her four psychopathic sons. De Niro went into action – first he was off to Arkansas, along with his tape-recorder, to perfect the accent. In the film he was a morphine addict, so he systematically starved himself, losing almost two stone before filming started. He broke out in sores, which he deliberately picked. The film itself was pure sleaze and panned by the critics, but once again De Niro was picked out for his very realistic characterisation.

Slowly, his career was beginning to move. Shelley Winters advised him to join the Boston Theater Company to gain more experience, and this he did, achieving good reviews.

De Niro's next part in *Bang the Drum Slowly* was for Paramount Pictures, and he had to undergo no less than seven auditions before getting the part. He played a somewhat stupid baseball catcher, who discovers that he has a progressive, malignant disease. Although it was not the lead role (the story was narrated by his best friend), he underwent rigorous training: first he perfected his accent, then spent several weeks learning all the tricks of baseball. During filming he pushed his fingers down his throat – forty times – in order to produce real tears. But for him, the worst part was learning how to chew tobacco and look as if he were enjoying it. Recognition came at last – his performance won him the New York Critics Award for Best Supporting Actor.

De Niro was now thirty. It had been a long haul, but he had never thought that anything would come easy, as his father's life, dedicated to painting and poverty, had amply demonstrated. Quietly and unassumingly, he continued his study of acting, never knowing if success was just round the corner.

# SUCCESS

A meeting at a party in the early 1970s was to change De Niro's fortunes. Martin Scorsese had grown up in 'Little Italy' in New York's Lower East Side, very near where De Niro had lived – in fact they had met as children – and when they met again they found they had much in common.

Scorsese was an up-and-coming director. His latest project was *Mean Streets*, set in the very streets where both had played as children.

Robert De Niro in *Mean Streets*

Their collaboration in this film would advance both their careers. Neither particularly liked the Hollywood system of having to have stars to front films – Scorsese was influenced by the French New Wave cinema, which focused on the whole film and the characterisation, and was not averse to using unknown actors. He invited De Niro to play Johnny Boy, a pathological maniac playing sidekick to a thrusting gangster (Harvey Keitel). De Niro knew the real-life 'punk bastard' Johnny Boy was based on. He talked to people who knew him, then used his own instinct to depict a streetwise character with a sort of rough sex appeal, but a loser.

The film showed a new kind of realism – menacing violence in ordinary, seedy streets – but luridly lit to give them a threatening surrealism. Tony's Bar, where much of the action takes place, was in fact a film set thousands of miles away in Hollywood.

The American public did not know quite how to take this new kind of realism, but De Niro's acting was hailed as 'wild and strong', 'intensely appealing', and was praised for its 'terrific pace and energy'.

He was offered a part in Frank Coppola's sequel to *The Godfather*, *The Godfather, Part II*, as Vito Corleone – in other words the part Marlon Brando had played so electrifyingly in the original film. It was a hard act to follow – or rather, precede – as this was to be the *young* Corleone seen in flashbacks. It needed research if De Niro was to play it with authenticity. Brando had given the *padrone* dignity, made him a family man. Coppola now wanted to redress the balance by highlighting his less

Playing a young Brando in *The Godfather, Part II*

attractive violent beginnings as a gangster, and
it was De Niro's task to reconcile these differ-
ences. He watched Brando's performance in
the original film over and over again, to catch
the nuances. He flew to Sicily, first visiting
Palermo, and then the small hill town of
Corleone, the very heart of mafia country,
where it had all started. These experiences
gave him the dimension of fear lacking in
Brando's interpretation: he found the Sicilians
covertly watching his every move. But it was
reciprocal, for he was tape-recording their
conversations and memorising their facial
gestures and expressions. The resulting performance was dazzling, and he won an Oscar for
Best Supporting Actor. Brando himself hailed
him as 'the most talented actor working
today', but recognising De Niro's self-effacing
modesty, added: 'I doubt if he knows how
good he is.'

De Niro was still living in a modest apartment in Greenwich Village and had a small circle of friends, mainly those he had met while acting. He fell in love with a young black actress, model and singer – Diahnne Abbott, who, temporarily jobless, was surviving as a waitress. She had a six-year-old daughter Drina from a previous marriage. The romance wasn't something that happened quickly – apart from the obvious physical attraction, she liked his quiet manner and his gentleness, and he was attracted by her commitment to her career. But it would blossom into a passionate relationship, although they were never possessive of each other and gave each other space.

After winning his Oscar for Vito Corleone in 1974, De Niro never looked back, apart from an abortive project with Mike Nichols – *Bogart Slept Here* – about an out-of-work actor. Nichols found De Niro 'undirectable', while De Niro found Nichols virtually impossible to work with.

His next film, Bertolucci's *Novecento*, had a different set of problems. A straggling epic with a communist message, it recounted the parallel lives of two boys: one (De Niro) born to wealthy landowners, the other (Gérard Depardieu) a poor peasant. Friends at first, in adulthood they find themselves on opposing political sides and their friendship turns to hatred. The film was peppered with bizarre sex scenes, from masturbation to sex with an epileptic girl. The film suffered from 'director's megalomania' – both Orson Welles and Maria Schneider walked out – and it became wildly overlength and overbudget, the director seemingly unable to stop his creative flow. Although De Niro admired Bertolucci's intensity, the two clashed (although they became firm friends later): Bertolucci found him sensitive but neurotic. The heavily edited end-product was unfortunately not a box office success.

Martin Scorsese's *Taxi Driver*, De Niro's next project, *was* a success even though that too went overbudget – by half a million dollars, and Scorsese recalls how he was constantly hassled by the studios. It is a film about urban loneliness, and a man who is driven crazy by it. De Niro plays an ex-marine, Travis Bickle, a shy loner who drives a cab by night, obsessively drawn to the city's pornographic night life; increasingly appalled by the world he sees but too timid to indulge in it, he unleashes a torrent of sickening violence.

De Niro's girlfriend Diahnne was given a

*Taxi Driver*, De Niro in the title role

small part – as a cinema usherette. He, as usual, submerged himself in his role. When they were discussing how he should play his role, De Niro asked Scorsese, 'What sort of animal would I be like?' Scorsese suggested, 'Why not a tiger?' 'No', De Niro said, 'I think I'd be more like a wolf, always on the lookout, watching.' So he went off to the zoo to study how a caged wolf behaved. Scorsese liked that – he has always liked actors who play by their instincts. De Niro also took to cab-driving at night for two weeks, only to find one fare recognising him: 'Jesus! Last year you won an Oscar, and now you're driving cabs! Guess it's hard to find steady work.'

De Niro played his part with utter conviction. His words, 'You talking at me? Are you talkin' to me?' as he addresses his lone reflection, are now part of film history. The reviews were stunning. The film made over $25 million at the box office, and was nominated for four Oscars.

One member of the public became obsessed with De Niro's role. He played the film over and over, 15 times, and came to think that he *was* Bickle, who at one time stalks a presidential candidate. The man's name was John Hinckley, and his intended victim the American president, Ronald Reagan.

Robert De Niro with Jeanne Moreau in
*The Last Tycoon*

# HOLLYWOOD

Despite De Niro's dislike for the razzmatazz of
Hollywood, his next film would not only take
him there, but would have Hollywood as its
subject. Most of his supporting cast would be
Hollywood stars too: Anjelica Huston, Jack
Nicholson, Tony Curtis, Robert Mitchum,
Donald Pleasance . . . The film was *The Last
Tycoon*, directed by Elia Kazan, who had been
Brando's idol and who had done more than
any other director of his generation to en-
courage Method acting in the film world. De

Niro did not want to miss the opportunity of working with him.

He and Diahnne moved to a rambling house in Bel-Air, having been banned from their hotel suite when it was discovered Diahnne had smuggled four cats inside.

Kazan had a hunch that De Niro would be right as Monroe Stahr, the young workaholic movie mogul who burns himself out in his thirties. Sam Spiegel, the producer, who had invested $5.5 million in the film, thought otherwise: De Niro was common, 'a petty larceny punk' lacking social graces. Added friction was caused by Kazan finding Harold Pinter's adaptation of Scott Fitzgerald's novel tedious and desperately in need of more action and love interest, and almost everyone, except Sam Spiegel, found the leading lady's beauty outshone her acting ability.

For De Niro it was an entirely new, challenging sort of role and he worked himself into it by walking the deserted lots at Paramount Studios in a three-piece suit and thinking 'This is all mine'. He dieted – losing three stone – to make himself look ambitiously thin. But, in the end, his part had little impact – he was too low key, and the love interest was weak.

Not so in his private life, for in June 1976 De Niro and Diahnne married quietly, in the presence of just a few friends. Diahnne was pregnant again, and their son Raphael (named after the Rome hotel where he was conceived) was born during the shooting of De Niro's next film.

*The Deer Hunter*

*The Last Tycoon* had not been a commercial success and a change of image was required. His friend Scorsese invited him to take the supporting role in a musical, *New York, New York*, set in the 1940s. His stage wife was the dynamic Lisa Minelli, seduced into a rocky marriage where, though both husband and wife are madly in love, they just can't live together. They separate and there is a final non-reunion in which they both walk away. Diahnne also had a part as a beautiful black singer. De Niro had fun learning the tenor saxophone for his role, though his music coach didn't. De Niro had insisted on three months' intense study, asking so many questions that his coach said 'working with De Niro was about as much fun as the clap'.

*New York, New York* was in stark contrast to *The Deer Hunter*, Michael Cimino's attempt to show how the Vietnam War impinged on ordinary Americans' lives, and in particular on a small community living near a steelworks. It depicts three men from that community drafted into the army and sent to Vietnam. They are captured by the Vietcong and subjected to horrendous torture, which damaged them emotionally and mentally for ever. For six weeks, De Niro went to live in the steel towns in Indiana, West Virginia, Pennsylvania and Ohio, eating, drinking and playing pool with the men, though none of the steelmills would allow him in to work.

The Vietcong torture includes an implausible, but controversial part where prisoners are forced to play Russian roulette. The tense and emotional scene of De Niro watching it happen was one of the most difficult he had to play in his career.

The film was shot in Thailand, and De Niro and fellow actor John Savage almost came to grief when they had to hang on to a helicopter 30 feet above the river Kwai, before falling into the water. The helicopter flew too low and took out a bridge, with them still clinging to it.

Meryl Streep had agreed to take a small part in the film because her lover John Cazale was playing one of the three men. Cazale had bone cancer and sadly died before it was released. Streep's part was enlarged and she played love scenes with De Niro – both impressed by the other's professionalism.

De Niro is a pivotal figure in the film and he felt it was the best performance he had ever given. He was nominated for an Oscar and the film was voted Best Motion Picture of the Year.

However, as a realistic picture of Vietnam it was sadly biased, and at the Berlin Film Festival, the Eastern bloc countries walked out: for them the film was an insult to the Vietnamese people.

In the spring of 1979, De Niro and Diahnne separated. Part of the problem was that De Niro was hardly ever at home – he spent much of the time away immersing himself in his various roles, and when he was at home the intensity of his role-playing made him extremely difficult, if not impossible, to live with. Diahnne had also decided that she actually liked Hollywood, whereas De Niro could not even bear to turn up for the Oscar ceremony – she now felt caged in by his obsessive need for privacy. While she stayed on in Hollywood, De Niro returned to New York, although they would continue to see each other and share holidays with the children. The marriage breakdown hurt him intensely. He told a friend that he could have been just as happy without the fame. 'I miss Di and the kids terribly. They are always on my mind . . .' But by this time De Niro had become involved with another woman: she was Toukie Smith, a black model described as 'a cyclone of dizzy charm'.

# LOVE INTEREST

Jake La Motta, known as the 'Bronx Bull', became World Middleweight boxing champion in 1949, then lost to Sugar Ray Robinson and went into a decline, ending up as a night club bouncer-cum-comic. De Niro happened to read his autobiography, and suggested it as a film to Scorsese. 'I was interested in fighters,' he said. 'The way they walk, the weight thing – they always blow up – and there was just something about La Motta . . . I wanted to play a fighter – just

37

like a child wants to be somebody else.'

This he would do in *Raging Bull*. It was truly challenging and required concentrated training. La Motta himself coached him – over four months they played a thousand rounds, so that by the time they came to shoot the film, La Motta declared that De Niro ranked in the top 20 middleweights in the world, and La Motta showed the freshly broken caps of his front teeth to prove it! La Motta's ex-wife found such an uncanny resemblance between De Niro and what had been her youthful husband that she offered to go to bed with him, but De Niro politely declined.

La Motta gone-to-seed in the second half of the film demanded a totally different portrayal. Filming was delayed while De Niro flew to Italy and fattened himself into dissolute

As Jake La Motta in *Raging Bull*

middle-age by stuffing himself with pasta – he put on 60 lbs and developed a bullneck. Such was the transformation that his daughter Drina was ashamed to be seen with him.

The film, shot in black and white, marks the high point in De Niro's achievement as an actor. Some may dislike it for its bestiality and seediness, but no one can deny its power and lack of compromise. By comparison, Stallone's Rocky looks almost soppy.

When filming was over, De Niro felt depressed and did not work for a year. He flew to Italy for a rest, but at Rome airport was held for questioning as an official had mistaken him for a terrorist!

After he had returned to New York, he saw an attractive girl in another car at the traffic lights one evening and decided to follow her. The girl was Helena Springs, a black singer who had done backing vocals for Bob Dylan, Eric Clapton, David Bowie and Elton John. Their chance encounter developed rapidly into a passionate affair, consummated the night before he won an Oscar for Best Actor for *Raging Bull*. The relationship would last off and on until 1992 when it ended on a distinctly sour note.

De Niro's next role was a far cry from his last: he played a worldly priest whose love of success outweighs his love of the church. His religious adviser on the film thought his portrayal 'the most authentic priest ever seen on screen'. Robert Duvall played his brother who has become a detective. But the public were apathetic about the film.

*True Confessions* was shot in Los Angeles where De Niro renewed his friendship with the comedian John Belushi, star of *Animal House*, who idolised him. Both frequented a night spot called On the Rox, a place where cocaine was rumoured to be frequently used. De Niro was with Belushi at his bungalow shortly before he died. The press made a great deal of this, and De Niro was devastated at the death of his close friend.

It was ironic that the subject of De Niro's next film should be about a would-be comedian, *King of Comedy*, made under Scorsese's direction again. De Niro plays a fan who desperately wants to escape his mundane existence and become a star. He succeeds in kidnapping a TV show host for a vital quarter of an hour while he performs his comedy act. And although taken off to prison, he writes his

autobiography and achieves fame. Jerry Lewis
played the TV host and thought De Niro 'the
ultimate professional'. De Niro refused to eat
lunch with Lewis during filming, as their characters were quarreling in the film. Many
thought De Niro too good for this part. The
film cost $20 million to make, but was a
turkey. In the meantime Helena had had a
baby, whom De Niro would adopt – Nina
Nadeja De Niro. But he was still married to
Diahnne and as yet there was no question of a
divorce – in fact she was working with him in
*King of Comedy*, as his occasional girlfriend!

For his part in *Once Upon a Time in America*,
directed by Sergio Leone, De Niro was
reputedly paid $2 million. The film tells the
long saga of gangsterdom in America from the
1920s to the1960s, and to give it authenticity,
it was agreed that the same actors should play

themselves at 20, 40 and 60 years old. But it was a lumbering, meandering film that ended up wildly overlength and overbudget. The editing job performed to make it into a commercial length film marred it.

In *Falling in Love*, also released in 1984, De Niro had a chance to act once again with Meryl Streep. The story, rather like *Brief Encounter* but set in a New York bookshop instead of a railway station, is about a suburban husband and a suburban wife who meet, fall in love and commit adultery. As in *Brief Encounter* the ending is unresolved. This was one of the few occasions where De Niro plays a romantic lead, and although both he and Streep gave sensitive performances, his character lacked the edge of the more macho roles his fans had come to expect, and they were disappointed.

De Niro had now entered his forties, a testing time for any actor. The next decade, like the curate's egg, promised to be good in parts.

# LIVING ON THE EDGE

Although only one film De Niro took part in in the late 1980s was a raging box office success, each of the characters he played showed his increasing diversity and range as an actor.

De Niro was a fan of *Monty Python*, so when one of the team, Terry Gilliam, was about to direct what he described as an 'Orwellian pantomime', De Niro thought it might be fun. *Brazil* was a satirical view of the future –

showing a world controlled by machines and bureaucracy. Bravely, De Niro was to play only a cameo role – as a repair man – while Jonathan Pryce played the lead as a victim of this Orwellian nightmare. But the film was fraught with problems and friction between producer and director. The result was not a happy one, and De Niro's image, after yet another box-office failure, was at a low ebb.

After this came a nightmare of another sort: Colombia – the gruelling setting for Roland Joffe's flawed masterpiece, *The Mission*, with a script by Robert Bolt. It was set in mid-18th-century South America, at a Jesuit mission in the jungle. Joffe cast De Niro as Mendoza, a slave trader who converts to Christianity and becomes a Jesuit priest, only to convert back to his former violence in a bid to save the native Indians from the Spanish terror. Joffe

The Mission, Mendoza and Father Gabriel

said of De Niro's performance: 'There wasn't anybody who had the inner complexity that Bob had [which] is there without him having to do anything – it's a part of his presence.'

They were on location for three months, and almost all the cast and crew went down with amoebic dysentery. The set was built above the breathtaking Iguaza Falls, but unfortunately it also turned out to be right in the path of a major cocaine-trafficking route out of the country, so that they were constantly surrounded by police patrols with machine-guns. Add to this, stifling humidity, violent downpours and flooding. De Niro grew his hair long and straggly for his part, and also sported a beard, which mightily impressed the native Indian extras. In the story he finds his brother with his mistress Carlotta, kills him, then confesses his crime to the pious Father

Gabriel (played by Jeremy Irons) who converts him. The acting styles of Irons and De Niro were, on the surface, incompatible. This caused problems at first, but after a while they could appreciate each other's differing points of view, and Irons described his fellow actor as 'a lovely man'.

Perhaps one of the most powerful sequences in the film is De Niro performing his self-inflicted penance: like a latter-day Sisyphus, he heaves his weighty armour up the slithery face of the Iguaza Falls, only to let it fall and start all over again.

The final scene where the Indians are slaughtered and the mission set ablaze was more real than intended; the set caught alight prematurely, and some of the crew and cast had to run for their lives. The look of horror on their faces was absolutely genuine.

The film won the Palme d'Or at Cannes Film Festival in 1986, but attracted very mixed reviews ranging from 'a truly embarrassing performance' to 'a magnificent achievement'. Basically, the film was far too long, and Warner Brothers lost a lot of money.

*The Mission* did, however, bring De Niro more fame, and his next role seems at first a somewhat bizarre choice – a cameo part in *Angel Heart*, directed by Alan Parker, a supernatural thriller set in New York's Lower East side in the 1950s, with voodoo, murder and walls dripping with blood. De Niro plays the Devil himself, masquerading as Lou Cifre (Lucifer), and plays him convincingly down to the last long fingernail. Parker was filled with admiration for De Niro's thorough approach and for his 'phenomenal involvement' but thought working with him through a whole film might be an 'exhausting' experience. The result was sinister and gory rather than entertaining and the public's reaction wasn't favourable.

After this De Niro took part in a stage play, *Cuba and his Teddy Bear*. He had not played in the theatre for some ten years and found it a restorative process, giving spellbinding performances as a drug-dealer and father of a son. He was now ready to tackle the film world again, and this time his old colleague Brian De Palma came up with a winner. De Niro would play Al Capone in *The Untouchables*, with a screenplay by David Mamet, and co-stars including Sean Connery and the then almost unknown Kevin Costner. Everyone was anxious to avoid the Hollywood cliché of showing gangsters as glamorous people, and

As Al Capone in *The Untouchables*

the part of Al Capone demanded subtlety. De Niro read all he could find on the subject and watched the few old newsreels in which he appeared. In order to get his physical appearance right he went on another trip to Italy to fatten up by two stone, and shaved the front of his hair to look as though he was balding. In real life Al Capone was a psychopath subject to violent temper tantrums, but he was also a charmer, an efficient businessman, and regarded by many as a benefactor for supplying illicit liquor during Prohibition. As an example of his obsessive perfectionism, De Niro wore silk underwear (like Al Capone) throughout the shooting; although it was invisible at all times, he said it helped him to feel like the man.

When the film was released, critics recognised De Niro's genius: 'Mesmerizingly intimidating' and 'icily murderous' are how they described him; Sean Connery had equal praise. In a rare press interview, De Niro described how he enjoyed playing evil men – they were more plausible and real. They lived life 'at the edge'.

# AWAKENINGS

The late 1980s mark a period of changing priorities for De Niro.

In 1987, he was invited to the USSR to head the jury at the Moscow Film Festival and, as a remarkable symbol of rapprochement, the festival opened with a showing of *The Deer Hunter* – De Niro was at pains to explain that it was an anti-war rather than an anti-communist film.

In the spring of 1987, Toukie Smith, who had remained a secret girlfriend of De Niro's for some eight years, was mourning the death of her brother, the fashion designer Willi Smith, who had died of AIDS. In a loyal move, De Niro agreed to participate in a TV information advertisement on AIDS.

Before his Moscow trip, De Niro was asked to play in a commercial comedy, *Midnight Run*, produced and directed by Martin Brest of *Beverly Hills Cop* fame. Handcuffed to co-star Charles Grodin, De Niro plays a bounty hunter returning a Mafia book-keeper to Los Angeles after he has embezzled his *compadres'* funds. Grodin had confessed to a phobia for aeroplanes, so the hilarious, cliff-hanging journey is undertaken by train, bus and car, with a bunch of thugs in hot pursuit. The film was a hit and De Niro says he had great fun making it.

Sheltering from pursuit, *Midnight Run*

He then returned to new York to begin working seriously on a project he had had in mind for some time – to create his own film centre and restaurant in TriBeCa, the neighbourhood where he now lived. Once an inner-city zone of factories and warehouses, it was fast becoming a fashionably artistic quarter. Although he was said to have been netting as much as $5 million a picture, having his own film company would not only give him artistic control, but would also give him a greater percentage of the profits. Others had tried this in the past – years before Marlon Brando had found it was not so easy as it looked, but more recently stars like Robert Redford, Bruce Willis, and Sylvester Stallone had made a great success of their ventures. It would take De Niro several years to get his idea off the ground. Although he was very comfortably off, it needed vast funding.

He and Diahnne had still not divorced and he was now contacted by Helena Springs again. Although he had adopted her daughter Nina, he had only seen the child once and had not offered any financial support. Helena had married and her husband, who loved the little girl, desperately wanted to adopt her so that they could become a proper family. De Niro refused, and also refused to contribute any funds towards her education, or to behave like a father to her.

Just as there was confusion in his private life, so his film career became directionless. He was a star who, because he stuck to his values, did not fit easily into the system – certainly not the Hollywood system at any rate. He took part in a number of inferior films, including *Jacknife*, an attempt to show the after-effects of the Vietnam war on a veteran who cannot adapt to normal life. It was a plodding film and many were surprised that he had accepted a role in it, but assumed he had seen it as a kind of echo of *The Deer Hunter*. Perhaps De Niro was anxious to raise funds for his TriBeCa project, and his next film, a remake of a 1950s comedy, *We're No Angels*, was probably taken on for the same reason.

After this he was able to part-buy a warehouse in Canal Street near his home for $7 million. A further 23 investors came up with almost $3 million more, although he still needed much much more to turn the warehouse into a going concern as part of his TriBeCa project.

Although the money was welcome – and needed – De Niro did not court big parts in commercial blockbusters just for the sake of money – far more important to him was the interest of the role, particularly if it offered a completely new experience. Penny Marshall's film *Awakenings* offered just such an opportunity. It was based on Oliver Sacks' account of a real-life experiment on Parkinson's Disease patients in a mental hospital who had sunk into a rigid, catatonic state, but who, when given the drug L-Dopa, suddenly emerged from their paralysis and began to talk and move around. Then, as the effects of the drug wore off, they once again reverted to their frozen postures and frozen minds. De Niro took the part of a patient, Leonard Lowe, while Robin Williams played the psychiatrist.

De Niro plays his part completely without expression or eye-contact, until he is suddenly brought to life by the drug in an awesome moment. *Awakenings* was filmed in a Brooklyn mental hospital, and although it was a senti-

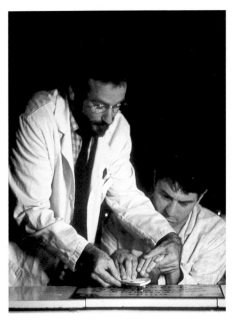

Psychiatrist and patient in *Awakenings*

mentalised version of real events and was given
an unreal, happy ending, it was nonetheless
extremely powerful and moving, and did
nothing but enhance De Niro's reputation.

Also in 1990, after ten years apart, De Niro
and Martin Scorsese decided to collaborate on
a new film, *GoodFellas*, (the tale of a real crim-
inal Henry Hill, a New York *mafioso* who
decides to turn state's evidence, and who, as a
witness, is helped to go into hiding by the
FBI). Nicholas Pileggi, who had written Hill's
biography, collaborated on the screenplay.
Many members of Scorsese's old team were
brought together for this production. Hill was
played by Ray Liotta, while De Niro played a
supporting role as Jimmy Conway, a cold-
blooded assassin, although, as usual, his role
became pivotal. It was a violent film, and
though not wildly received at the time, it has

De Niro in *GoodFellas*

now come to be recognised as exceptionally good.

De Niro, now in his mid-forties, was then to star for the first time with Jane Fonda in a film variously called *Stanley and Iris* and *Letters from Vietnam*. He plays a worker in a cake factory who is sacked because he cannot read or write; Jane Fonda acts as his teacher. Implausibly, Stanley then becomes a successful businessman and asks Iris to marry him. It was not a successful film at the box office.

De Niro now faced new problems. Although the film centre project was going ahead, he had to contend with picketing neighbours, worried about the adverse effects his project might have on the locality. As well as this, Helena Springs had divorced, and once again asked De Niro to take some part in their daughter's life, and to start behaving like a father. Although he did make some provision, at this stage he still took little interest. In the meantime Diahnne was quietly pursuing their divorce, while a new girlfriend had made her appearance: supermodel Naomi Campbell.

# MAKE OR BREAK

At the beginning of the 1990s, De Niro earned nearly $20 million for six fairly indifferent films. *Guilty of Suspicion* was set in 1950's Hollywood, at the time of Senator McCarthy's witch-hunt of communist sympathisers. De Niro plays a blacklisted actor. In *Backdraft* in the same year, he has a supporting role as a fire investigator.

While making *Backdraft*, De Niro renewed his relationship with Helena Springs. It is through

Helena's eyes that we are able to glimpse a little of De Niro's private life: 'He was always a fantastic lover,' she said, 'but I also know that he has tons of women.' De Niro confessed that 'women just throw themselves at me.' However, Helena now wanted De Niro either to behave like a father or to get out of her life – an ultimatum that would have sad repercussions – but for the moment he refused to decide one way or the other.

*Cape Fear*, a remake of a 1962 film of the same name, was to be a joint production by Steven Spielberg and De Niro's own company TriBeCa. Spielberg had to pull out, so Martin Scorsese took over the direction. De Niro, however, retained a fair amount of control – but by then the plot had already been forced into an unsuitably commercial mould. It is generally agreed that De Niro's performance was overdone. His next production, *Mistress*, was one of his least memorable and sank without trace.

According to some, De Niro and Toukie Smith had at one stage been preparing to get married, but Naomi Campbell was still in the picture. Then, early in 1992, De Niro began to take a real interest in Helena's daughter Nina. He invited her to Vancouver for a weekend and afterwards phoned her frequently. Nina, now ten years old, was thrilled that at last she was getting to know her father. But Helena wanted the relationship to be put on a firmer footing. De Niro agreed, but only on condition that Nina had a blood test to prove his paternity. After all this time, to Helena's utter amazement, the test proved that De Niro was not Nina's father. (The only other contender had been drowned in a

As the police photographer, *Mad Dog and Glory*

boating accident years before). However, Helena was advised by her lawyer that despite the blood test, there was a good chance that she could still claim maintenance since De Niro had adopted Nina, had for many years accepted her as his own without question, and had obstructed her adoption by Helena's husband. The court case, which Helena and Nina eventually lost, rumbled on for several years. They lost on the grounds that 'no bonding' had taken place between Nina and De Niro, as De Niro had had minimal involvement. Therefore he was not obliged 'legally, morally or ethically' to support her.

In the meantime, De Niro made another film, *Night and the City* – another remake – using his own production company. The film was about wrestling and was not a wild success. His next venture – *Mad Dog and Glory* – about a police

65

photographer, was also generally regarded as second-rate. The consensus was that he was taking on too many small-budget pictures, and making them too quickly.

De Niro's next picture, however, *This Boy's Life*, for Warner Brothers, was better. It was directed by Michael Caton-Bell who had directed *Scandal*. De Niro played an autocratic stepfather to a delinquent son, and Caton-Bell could not get over the intense perfectionism with which De Niro approached a role – for instance trying on 200 jackets to find one that felt just right.

But the tide was beginning to turn against De Niro: he was not expanding his range the way some of his fellow actors had, like Dustin Hoffman and Jack Nicholson. Instead, again and again, he drew inspiration from his New

Bus driver De Niro and his screen son, Francis Capra, *A Bronx Tale*

York background, and went on to make *A Bronx Tale* which he directed and starred in. It was a tale of childhood and growing up in an Italian community in the Bronx, where old-fashioned values clash with the crime world. He gave his usual impeccable performance – as a bus driver this time – but directing was fraught with problems. Originally, Universal Pictures were backing the film, but because of De Niro's meticulous approach, it ran over budget. His own company was then obliged to take over the production and find new backers, but it continued to go wildly over even the new budget – creeping up from the original $16 million to $24 million and ultimately producing nearly four miles of film for editing.

De Niro was now fifty. In May 1993, his father died. De Niro had genuinely cared for him, even hanging his paintings in his restaurant, and they were often seen eating there together.

*A Bronx Tale* had its first showing at the Venice Film Festival that spring to a standing ovation. It made a loss but was well received by the critics, and showed a new dimension to De Niro's skills.

In 1993 De Niro also became the Creature in Kenneth Branagh's *Mary Shelley's Frankenstein*. Both Branagh and De Niro wanted to veer away from earlier film versions and follow Mary Shelley's concept – 'horrific but capable of inspiring sympathy'. De Niro also wanted the film to be intelligent and angry, and spent nine months preparing for the role. But the over-hyping put off the critics and public alike; in the end it did little for De Niro's reputation.

De Niro was back on course with the release of *Heat*. Stylishly directed by Michael Mann, this 'urban Western' follows an obsessive detective (Al Pacino) in his relentless hunt for McCauley (De Niro), a cold-blooded gangster. De Niro and Pacino make an effective duo in an albeit implausible scene when they sip coffee together (supposedly based on a true incident). This is followed by what must be the longest and loudest shoot-out ever. McCauley has vowed that there will be nothing in his life he can't walk away from in 30 seconds, and proves it, with the subtlest and briefest of hesitations, as he leaves his girlfriend to walk into Pacino's final trap. The film ends on a highly sentimental note as the dying De Niro and Pacino hold hands in what must be the ultimate symbol of male bonding.

Scarcely a month after *Heat* came *Casino*,

Robert De Niro in *Casino*

directed by his old friend Martin Scorsese, and using scriptwriters and some of the actors, like the brilliantly sinister Joe Pesci, straight from *GoodFellas,* along with the Mid-West mob. *Casino* reflects the last blast of organised crime before Las Vegas became a family-friendly sort of place. De Niro plays Ace, the Mafia casino boss who falls for  high-class hustler (Sharon Stone), only to lose her to his murderous friend (Pesci). De Niro, Pesci and Stone all give brilliant performances, even if the back-drop may seem well-trodden ground.

Meanwhile the relationship with Naomi Campbell floundered, as did his relationship with Toukie Smith.

Three more films starring De Niro are also promised for 1996 – *The Fan*, *Marvin's Room* and *Sleepers*. Will they break the mould once again? Or will his future turn now towards directing?

On that, and on his private life, De Niro remains as taciturn as ever.

# FILMOGRAPHY

The year refers to the first release date
of the film

1966   Trois Chambres à Manhattan
1968   Greetings
1969   The Wedding Party
1969   Sam's Song
1969   Hi, Mom!
1969   Bloody Mama
1971   Jennifer On My Mind
1971   Born to Win
1971   The Gang That Couldn't Shoot
       Straight
1973   Bang the Drum Slowly

The Creature in *Mary Shelley's Frankenstein*

| 1973 | Mean Streets |
|------|-------------|
| 1974 | The Godfather, Part II |
| 1976 | Novecento (aka 1900) |
| 1976 | Taxi Driver |
| 1976 | The Last Tycoon |
| 1977 | New York, New York |
| 1978 | The Deer Hunter |
| 1980 | Raging Bull |
| 1981 | True Confessions |
| 1983 | King of Comedy |
| 1984 | Once Upon a Time in America |
| 1984 | Falling in Love |
| 1985 | Brazil |
| 1986 | The Mission |
| 1987 | Angel Heart |
| 1987 | The Untouchables |
| 1988 | Midnight Run |
| 1989 | Jacknife |
| 1989 | We're No Angels |
| 1990 | Awakenings |